EASY RAMBLES

AROUND
ENNERDALE
AND THE
CALDER VALLEY

MARY WELSH

QUESTA

ISBN 978-1-898808-31-2

Maps:

Published by
Questa Publishing Limited
27 Camwood, Bamber Bridge,
Lancashire PR5 8LA

and printed by
Carnmor Print, 95/97 London Road, Preston,
Lancashire PR1 4BA

CONTENTS

Introduction	5
1 Thornholme	8
2 Monks Bridge	11
3 Flat Fell	13
4 Dent Fell	16
5 Ennerdale Water West	19
6 Ennerdale Water and the Anglers' Inn	22
7 Cogra Moss (Short walk)	25
8 Cogra Moss South	27
9 Smithy Beck Forest Trail	29
10 Liza Beck	32

NOTE

No attempt has been made to grade the walks in this book, as this is too subjective. Use the information about distance and height gain to calculate how long the walk will take.

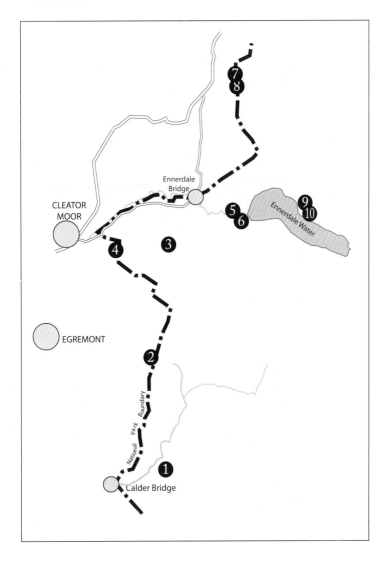

INTRODUCTION

Ennerdale Bridge, the village, stands at the foot of one of the loneliest of Lakeland's great valleys. It grew up at the point where the valley road crosses the River Ehen and meets the roads, south over Cold Fell and north from Kirkland.

Few people, today, depend on farming in Ennerdale Bridge, but they are constantly reminded of their agricultural past, by the drystone walls on the surrounding fells, the in-bye fields and pastures, well maintained by the local farmers. Once, the valley was full of activity with haematite ore mined on both sides of the lake. Iron was smelted beside Smithy Beck at the head of the lake and the remnants of the site are visited in walk nine of this book.

Today Ennerdale is a quiet remote dale, enjoyed by walkers who are looking for peaceful rambles and who like to have the lovely countryside almost entirely to themselves. It is a long valley gouged out by a glacier during the Ice Age. The head of valley is composed of granophyre, a hard volcanic rock, the foot is of friable Skiddaw Slates, which allowed the glacier to splay out widening the lower end of the lake.

The deepest part of lake is over 40m/130ft deep. The water is clear and pure, supporting little life except for brown trout, char – a relic of the Ice Age – and salmon passing through on their way to spawn.

Since the middle of the 19th century, Ennerdale Water has been used to provide water for West Cumbria, and in 1864 a shallow weir was created. In 1960, there were plans to raise the level of the lake to get extra water for industry. In preparation for this, in 1961, the famous shoreline Anglers' Inn was demolished. Raising of the level never materialised and the inn was demolished needlessly.

A delightful path leads from the Bleach Green car park to the site of the old inn and then continues along the shore to reach the car park at Bowness Point. This car park is accessed by a narrow lane from Ennerdale Bridge via Croasdale. The view of the lake and the fells is spectacular from here. No vehicles are allowed beyond the parking area.

Higher up the valley sweeping conifer plantations line the slopes and one of the walks in this book takes you through the forest, keeping mainly beside the delightful River Liza before it flows into the lake. It is a pleasing ramble especially on a wild, windy, winter's day and there are many glimpses of the dramatic slopes of Steeple, Pillar, Red Pike and other nearby fells.

Above the forest is the dale head where the land opens out. Here lonely, remote Black Sail, the highest youth hostel in Cumbria, is situated. This is the starting point for dedicated walkers to reach the summits of some of the most majestic fells in the Lake District. Less ambitious walkers may still enjoy climbing the long track and then the path to the hostel. But it is beyond the remit of this book as is completing the 11.4km (7-mile) circuit of the lake. Here the path across the rugged cliff of Anglers' Crag is quite exposed and, after rain, becomes very slippery – into the lake!

The first two walks in this book take you beside the River Calder, which rises on Kinniside Common. The waters of Whoap Beck, Stinking Gill and Comb Beck come together, high on bleak moorland, to form the river. It then gathers more water from the Mosses as it travels south, tumbles down Gill Force and then soon flows under the finest packhorse bridge, Monks Bridge, in Cumbria. Above Thornholme farm, Worm Gill joins the Calder.

The river hurries on past picturesque Calder Abbey. It has a fine tower, lofty walls and fine arches and was a daughter monastic house of Furness Abbey. It was founded in 1134 as a Benedictine monastery, which 14 years later joined the Cistercians. It survived until 1536, when it was dissolved on the orders of Henry VIII. English Heritage has done considerable work on the abbey to make the structures safe. The abbey is on private land and if you wish to visit you should write to the custodian at Abbey House, Calder Bridge, Cumbria to make an appointment to be shown around. Failing that you can see much of the abbey across a pasture from a nearby footpath, which starts from Calder Bridge and continues, delightfully, by the River Calder to the 'viewing' path.

The river flows through the village named after it, Calder Bridge. It once was a mainly agriculture community and then British Nuclear Fuels (BNFL) on the Sellafield site moved here in 1952 and to Calder Hall in 1956, employing many people from the village. From here the lovely long river after flowing through the dramatic lonely fells goes on to the sea, passing through Sellafield.

1

THORNHOLME

This is a most satisfactory walk, which takes you through fine deciduous woodland in the valley of the River Calder, onto slopes above the wide, dancing river. Near Thornholme, a charming isolated farmhouse, you cross the river and a beck and then return on an airy fell road, gated and unfenced for much of the way. The National Park has put in good stiles and a footbridge, and the route is well waymarked.

Start/Finish: Lay-by just beyond Stakes Bridge (NY056067). To reach this parking area, leave the A595 by a right turn at Calder Bridge. In just over half-a-mile where the road turns sharp left, continue ahead along a narrow 'No through road'.
Distance: 6.5km (4 miles)
Height gain: 60m (195ft)
Difficulty: Generally easy walking.

1. From the parking area, return over Stakes Bridge. Walk on for a few steps to take a signposted path, on the right, into Calder Woodlands. Stroll the delightful track through oak, beech and hazel. Where the track divides, keep to the right branch that keeps you well above the river. As you continue watch out for the waymark, directing you left, uphill on a narrow path, through the trees.

2. Follow the path to a stile on the edge of the trees. Beyond, bear right and follow the wall, then a fence, on your right. As you near the corner and the fence bears left, cut across the corner (to avoid a muddy hollow) and carry on with the continuing fence to your right. At the next corner, climb the stile and drop down the slope carefully. Cross a small beck and climb up to a stile.

3. Press on along the stiled and gated way, and enjoy the extensive view of the fells ahead. Watch out for the stile on your right, which gives access to a fenced track. Carry on with a fence to the right. Ignore the footpath that drops steeply downhill to the river. Continue ahead with the hedge to your left.

4. Just beyond the farm gate on the left watch for the track leaving the hedge and beginning its gentle descent, through scattered gorse. Pass through the gate and go on down to a sheepfold. Here follow the path as it swings left and climbs up the slope to a stile in the fence. Once over, walk ahead. Beyond the fence on the right the land drops steeply down to the hurrying river.

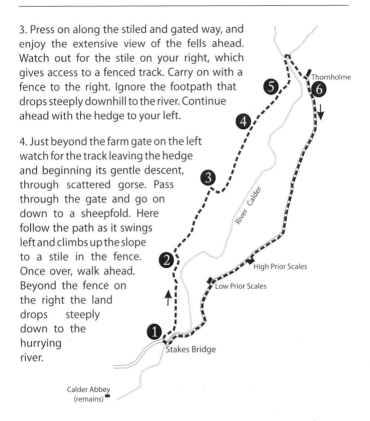

5. Continue over the next stile and follow the path as it drops down to a footbridge over the river, which you cross. Walk ahead, pass through the gate on your left and cross the next bridge over Worm Gill. Ascend the clear stony track, passing to the right of Thornholme farmhouse. At the fell road, turn right and climb the hill. From the brow you can see the towers of Sellafield.

6. Stride the gated fell road as it steadily descends. Look across the

deep valley of the Calder to see where you walked earlier. Go on to pass High Prior Scales farm. Here look for a modern barn for storing hay, which you pass first, and then the much older barn built of warm red stone, with exceptionally thick walls. Look for the carved face high on the building and the pigeon loft. Stroll on along the quiet road, passing Lower Prior Scales as you go, until you can join your car.

> *Notice the wall along the roadside. It is composed of two rows of Eskdale granite, a pinkish rock, which is rough to touch and which weathers to rounded cobbles. Look for the squarer boulders (throughs), which tie the two sides together.*

You may be tempted to lengthen this walk, or wish to add part of Walk 2 to it. If so, after crossing the first footbridge over the River Calder, near Thornholme, turn left onto a path, which winds right, round the side of a large knoll. The way soon becomes a wide rising track before descending as a wide grassy swathe, much enjoyed by sheep. This path was used by iron-ore carrying packhorses on their way to the Monks Bridge (the latter used when the ford lower downstream would have been too difficult to cross). Do not go over the footbridge across the Calder, at the foot of the incline, but follow the path upstream as described in walk two to see the packhorse bridge gem.

> *The Lake District is the largest of England's National Parks. It lies on the north west coast and is the wettest part of the country. Is this large quantity of rain that has been responsible for its 16 lakes and many tarns. It also receives gale force winds. These occur more often on the fell tops and coastal areas. Its several long beautiful valleys are much more sheltered. This walk through the valley of the River Calder is a good choice for a windy day, the route being well sheltered by the hills that enclose it.*

2

MONKS BRIDGE

This short walk takes you to a small hollow in the moorland of Kinniside Common where there is an easily missed magnificent packhorse bridge, one of the finest in Cumbria. It spans a young, narrow but impetuous River Calder. In summer the banks of the river are lined with bushes, trees and other rampant vegetation that almost hides its glory.

Start/Finish: A signed track going off east from Cold Fell Road, half way between Calder Bridge and Ennerdale Bridge. (NY055101). A National Trust board stands by a suitable parking area.
Distance: 3.5km (2 miles)
Height gain: 60m (195ft) on the return to the parking area.
Difficulty: The track to the bridge over the Calder is a delight to walk. A little scrambling is required to reach the packhorse bridge and after rain expect lots of mud here.

---

1. Walk the reinforced track, with Friar Gill to your right. Ignore a left branch and carry on down with pleasing views of the extensive moorland ahead and, beyond, the Lakeland hills. Wind round the wrought-iron barrier bar and continue down the now lush grassy track, much favoured by sheep.

2. Cross a small stream and carry on through a gate. Beyond are several small sheep pens on either side of the track. Then cross the river on a sturdy footbridge. Pause here to enjoy the view up and downstream.

3. Bear right for two steps and then take, left, a grassy trod, between rushes, keeping above the river. This leads slightly right and brings

you to a shallow crossing over Capleccrag Beck using well placed stones. Continue on the clear path and, in two or three steps, look down on the bridge. To reach it, weave a very short way down through rushes.

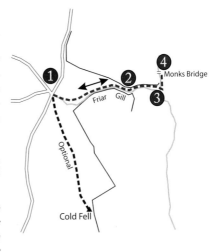

4. After a pause here, return by your outward route.

> *Monks Bridge arches like a fairy bridge, across a narrow chasm. It is just wide enough for a string of packhorses to cross. The monks of Calder abbey most likely built it – an easy job after the abbey – to use when the ford downstream was impassable. Iron ore would have been carried over the bridge from Ennerdale, to bloomeries or smithies, on the fells to be smelted. The bridge is also known as Matty Benn's bridge and sometimes Hannah Benn's. The Benn families lived nearby. Its other name is High Wath, meaning high ford.*

The slope to your right as you start your walk to Monks Bridge is Cold Fell (293m/960ft). If you have a little time to spare after your visit you might like to cross the cattle grid by the parking area and turn left along a track. Immediately take a faint path off right, which soon fades, and slant uphill towards the highest point of the fell. The view of the Calder Valley and Worm Gill are very pleasing and well worth making the airy ascent. Return by your outward route.

3

FLAT FELL

This is a pleasant walk, and although it does not have a view of Ennerdale Water, it passes through some spectacular countryside on easy-to-walk footpaths and tracks. It is quiet walking, just what Ennerdale is well known for.

Start/Finish: From verge below stone circle on Scarny Brow (NY059141). This is reached from Ennerdale Bridge village or by the road over Cold Fell
Distance: 6 km (3½ miles)
Height gain: 110m (360ft)
Difficulty: Generally easy walking on mostly reinforced paths and tracks.

This is a walk that takes you over the lower slopes of aptly named Flat Fell. It also takes you along three splendid valleys, formed during the last ice age by glacial action.

1. Cross the road from the verge and turn left for a few steps. Do not continue to the footpath sign but turn acute right, a few metres before it, back along a good track. Follow this downhill to reach another track, a wider one, where you turn left. Go on down between steep grassy slopes. Cross shallow Nannycatch Beck on stones and carry on. Where the path divides, take the more obvious track, on the right, and wind on round into a pleasing valley, with Flat Fell towering to the left.

2. Remain on the track as it climbs steadily towards a gate, a wall and several hawthorn trees, and then winds left. Continue on the pitched way as it curves right beside the fence on the right, with ever-increasing superb views across the Cumberland Plain, limestone

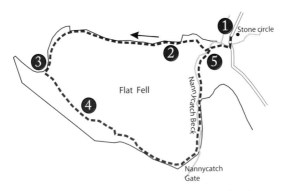

quarries and Meadley reservoir. Press on gently, up the sheep pasture of the north side of Flat Fell rising almost imperceptibly to summit on your left. The right-of-way continues to the brow of the track and then begins to descend into a boggy hollow beside the wall, and remains boggy as it descends. Better to keep parallel with, but away from the wall, following a distinct narrow grassy path dropping gently towards the conifers of Uldale Plantation.

3. On reaching a track, in the valley between Flat Fell and Dent Fell, well before the trees, turn left and continue on left with the south-west slopes of Flat Fell now on your left and the tree-clad slopes of Dent Fell to your right.

4. Press on along the bridleway, which is in good repair at first but then as it proceeds through the austere valley, an accompanying beck, after rain, leaves its bed and makes use of the track for a short stretch. Eventually the slopes close in; on the left the southern tip of Flat Fell and to the right, Raven Crag. Then you arrive at the charming hollow of Nannycatch Gate. Do not go through the gate ahead, but wind left on a good track, with Nannycatch Beck tumbling noisily beside you. Continue up the lovely valley. Pass below Flatfell Screes on your left. Cross several little streams hurrying to join the beck after descending the slopes on your right.

5. Eventually you join your outward path. Turn right and wind on up the track, until you reach the reinforced track, turning sharply back, right, which takes you up to the road. Cross and turn left to rejoin your vehicle.

The stone circle has a rather strange history. In the last century, so the story goes, the holes where the stones once stood were empty. A local farmer who was interested in stone circles scoured the countryside for stones that would fit the holes. He found them in stone walls, in buildings, some being used for other things. Eventually he managed to bring them back to the site and put them in place. No one quite knows whether it is a true stone circle or one created recently. But when the mist drifts over the moorland where the circle stands it seems very genuine.

This fine walk on the edge of Lakeland explores one of the lovely secret valleys of Cumbria. It is the crystal clear stream, Nannycatch Beck, that makes it so charming. While walking, look out for a dipper frequenting the rapids and cascades of the rapidly moving beck. It is a rotund short-tailed bird, dark above and white breasted. It might be seen sitting on a rock, round which water swirls, bobbing up and down, before plunging into the water, with a splash, to 'fly' beneath it, to obtain larvae of aquatic insects and other small creatures.

4

DENT FELL

You will have seen Dent Fell as you walked around Flat Fell (Walk 3). It has two fine viewpoints and the approach to the summit is by a very pleasant wide grassy swathe, after your ascent through the forest. It is part of the Northern Coast-to-Coast Walk and considering how much it is used, it shows little erosion.

Start/Finish: Park at the head of Nannycatch road (NY042139), where there are several lay-bys, or in a large space before the start of the forest road. Take care not to block access to the forest road. Nannycatch Road can be accessed from Egremont, Cleator Moor or Ennerdale Bridge.
Distance: 6km (4 miles)
Height gain: 190m/660ft
Difficulty: The track used for descent from below Dent fell to Nannycatch valley is long and heavily reinforced – but it does go down. The way through the valley and the return along the bridleway can be wet in parts after heavy rain.

---

1. From where you have parked, walk up the forest road (a good track) through trees. After less than 400m you reach a division of tracks. Leave the main one and take the narrower track/path on the right. Climb for a short way then wind left where the track becomes less steep. It then rises again before contouring along the slopes of Dent. Soon the path leads out onto open fell, clear-felled some years ago, allowing heather and bright green ferns to thrive. Across to the left, you can see Flat Fell and down below, the bridleway to Nannycatch Gate, part of Walk 3.

2. Continue on to reach a signpost for the Coast–to-Coast route, at a

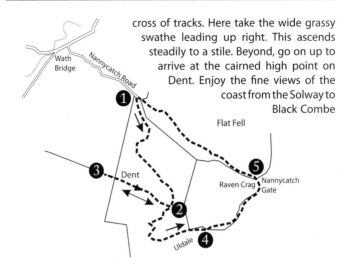

cross of tracks. Here take the wide grassy swathe leading up right. This ascends steadily to a stile. Beyond, go on up to arrive at the cairned high point on Dent. Enjoy the fine views of the coast from the Solway to Black Combe

and across to the Isle of Man. You might also be able to spot the fells around Ennerdale, and a tiny glimpse of the lake itself, and perhaps a misty silhouette of the Scafells and the Galloway coast. From here it is just a short way along the trod to the next high point, just 12m lower and again with superb views.

> On the slopes of Dent Fell where the forest has been clear-
> felled, heather is now thriving. Pause as you walk to look
> at its flowers. In summer these are pale pink or white. For
> nine or ten months after the flowers have opened they
> are still present, preserving much of their original form
> but very much bleached. Heather is also called ling.

3. Return to the cross of tracks and the signpost. Here turn right and, a short way along, turn left and follow the descending track, which runs beside the conifers of the plantation on your left. The track continues dropping steadily and then makes a steep zigzag and then a wider one, finally descending more easily to join a wider track, where you turn left. Carry on a short way to join another track and turn left

again. At this point look for a gate on the left that gives access to a footpath.

4. Walk the narrow grassy path to ford the narrow beck and then, if there has been heavy rain, you may have to ford it again where the beck has found a secondary route. Carry on, soon to cross the beck again, this time on a plank footbridge. Then cross the beck again on a railed plank bridge and carry on the clear way to take another. Cross the next railed footbridge directly below the spectacular Raven Crag, its slopes covered in interesting vegetation. Beyond, wind round left of the huge crag to go through the gate at Nannycatch Gate.

5. Stroll on ahead along the bridleway, passing between Flat Fell on the right and the steep northern grassy slopes of a spur of Dent fell. (If you have already completed Walk 3 you will have traversed this path in the opposite direction.) After heavy rain this will be a wet walk but as it rises, imperceptibly, the way becomes a track and has had some reinforcement. Carry on until you reach the wall coming down on your right from Flat Fell. Wind a little left along a wide track, which quickly brings you to a gate onto Nannycatch Road, where you have parked.

> After your walk, return down Nannycatch Road to join the road to Cleator Moor. Turn left, and in 330m you reach the charming two arched Wath Bridge over the River Ehen, four miles after it has issued forth from Ennerdale Water. There is a large lay-by for parking just beyond the bridge, on the B-road, and close by are seats and grassy flats from where to enjoy this attractive corner of West Cumbria.

5

ENNERDALE WATER WEST

From this delightful walk along the western shoreline of Ennerdale Water there are spectacular views of the mountains that shelter the head of the lake. The second part of the walk is slightly inland and involves a little road walking and a footpath across pastureland before returning along the edge of the lake once again.

Start/Finish: Bleach Green car park (NY086154) at the end of the signed road leading from Ennerdale Bridge village to the lakeshore.
Distance: 7km (4½ miles)
Height gain: Virtually none
Difficulty: Returning across the pasture to the lakeshore might be soggy after a long period of rain.

1. Leave by the gate at the far end of the car park to join a good surfaced path leading to the shore. Have your cameras ready for the superb view of the mountains over the shimmering water. Cross the footbridge, left, over the River Ehen, just after it has tumbled over a weir and then hurried on into lush vegetation. Carry on along the track through scrub vegetation to reach an open area of grass, the site of the Anglers' Inn, where it is possible to park (see below for directions). This is especially convenient for those who use wheelchairs and wish to travel a short way by the lake along the well-surfaced track provided by the National Trust (NT).

In his book 'The English Lakes', published in 1954, Frank Singleton describes the Anglers' Inn as follows: "The famous old inn stands so close (to the lake) that there is only room to walk past and the water laps beneath

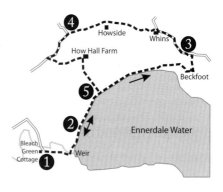

the windows in a way of which one could never tire. The situation of the inn is unique. As with Venice one hardly believes until one sees it. For this immediate foreground the mountains provide a noble setting. Ennerdale Water has a strange beauty of its own. It has no islands, and the outlines of the flanking hills are bare, but towards it centre, Angling Crag on the right and Bowness Knotts opposite, both beautiful crags, fall from higher fells and narrow the lake with fine and interesting effect".

2. Follow the lovely way until you reach a gate ahead, where an arrow directs you sharp right along the curving shore of the lake. Here you might wish to continue but this walk ignores the shore path and goes ahead up a pleasing, unsigned, wide, grassy hedged track. Go past Beckfoot, a NT house, and continue, left, on the track until you can join a road.

3. Turn left and ascend, with care along the narrow hedge-lined way until just past Whins, a gaunt farmhouse. Just beyond, take a left turn, which is metalled but very narrow, and has a sign, 'Unfit for vehicles'. This old lane, known as the 'Five-foot road' by locals, has hedges on either side and is a pleasure to walk. It climbs gently to pass Howside farm and then descends steadily, becoming a little wider to join a quiet road to Ennerdale Bridge from where there are good views across the lake to Anglers' Crag.

Today's maps use the names, Anglers' Crag and Bowness

Knott for the crags mentioned above. See the Walk 6 for the fate of the Anglers' Inn and the reason for it.

4. Walk left for 280m, and then turn left along the access track to How Hall farm. Just before the farm buildings, look for an unsigned gate, on the right, partly obscured by farm machinery. Pass through the gate and take a stile over the fence on the right. Descend a few steep grassy steps down the banking and then walk ahead, bearing slightly left over a pasture to an obvious gate (waymarked on the far side). Then press on ahead through an area of cut rushes to reach a fence at the bottom of the field to avoid a very wet area of rush further left. Turn left and walk with the fence to your right. Ignore a stile over the fence, and then a gate across a little sike, and go on ahead, still with the fence to your right, to take a gate ahead in a fence that encloses scattered trees. Walk ahead through the copse to reach the lakeshore.

5. Turn right, pass through a gate and retrace your outward path, enjoying a last view of the lovely lake and the surrounding mountains. Cross the footbridge over the Ehen and walk right to take the gate, on the right, into the end of the car park.

As you walk beside Ennerdale Water you might disturb a heron, which has been standing patiently in the shallows or on a little bank on the shore. It uses its pick-axe beak upon any unsuspecting fish, frog or beetle. As it flies away notice that its head is drawn back and its long legs are trailing. Herons nest in colonies, huge platforms with shallow cups, in the branches of tall trees. Large sticks are used with smaller but seldom soft material for lining. A few weeks after the eggs are laid the heronry is a livelsy place with half-naked nestlings with blint bills and stout lead-coloured legs.

6

ENNERDALE WATER AND THE ANGLERS' INN

This delightful walk takes in more of the shoreline of Ennerdale Water. It passes a ruined mill and then goes on past a farm with a wonderful history. Finally it comes to the site of the Anglers' Inn, which had a magnificent view up the lake, before it was demolished, unnecessarily. The site of the Inn is now a parking area, approached by the track (plus two gates) past the farmhouse. The National Trust have greatly improved the path along the shore for use by wheelchair users.

Start/Finish: Bleach Green car park (NY086154);
for access see Walk 5.
Distance: 6.5km (4 miles)
Height gain: Virtually none
Difficulty: Easy, but after heavy rain the paths on the south side of the River Ehen can be wet. Some quiet road walking.

---

1. Leave the car park by the far left corner and walk the little track, through trees, with the Ehen racing over its weir. Join the main track to the shore and go on ahead. Here notice the weir that controls the flood from the lake to the river. Ignore the footbridge on the left and bear right along the shore, using either of two paths. Cross a footbridge and go on to pass through a kissing gate in the wall.

2. Walk right, with the wall to your right, along a narrow path. Step across the wide shallow bed, of the beck that tumbles down Ben Gill. Ignore any gates on your right and carry on over a stile and on along a wide grassy ride, with the forest to your left and Scots pine to your right, a lovely sheltered corridor. Pass through a gate ahead, and go

on until you reach the point where the wall turns sharp right and runs down towards the river.

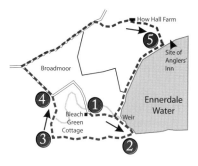

3. Turn right, beyond the wall, to walk a wide grassy ride to reach a gate/stile. Beyond, descend a sometimes wet path, to reach a very fine footbridge over the wide River Ehen. Take care on the ancient sandstone steps as you climb and descend the modern footbridge. Beyond, walk ahead to pass a house on the right, with evocative ruins of an old mill, behind. Join a track and wind left. Go through a gate, with a walkers welcome sign, to reach the signposted corner of the road from the car park. Here you might spot a red squirrel sitting on top of the post.

4. Stroll, left, along the quiet tree-lined road to a junction. Go right along a wider road, with a magnificent view ahead, for a kilometre, to take a signposted right turn. This leads to attractive How Hall farm (this lane traversed in Walk 5).

> *How Hall Farm stands on the reinforced track leading to the site of the Anglers' Inn. The plaque on the end wall of the barn is very weather worn but you can just read the following: 'This house was built AD1566 by Anthony Partickson and Frances, his wife, daughter of Sir Thomas Swinburne one of the Privy Council to King Henry VIII.'*

5. Remain on the continuing track, to pass in front of the house. Look on the far side of the last barn, which faces onto the road, to see an interesting but much eroded plaque. Then descend gently to go through a gate across the reinforced way. Follow the track as it bears right and goes on down through pastures to reach another gate. Beyond, the track slants left to join the shore path.

6. Walk ahead for a short way to a large open area and the remnants of a jetty jutting into the lake. This was the site of the Anglers' Inn demolished in 1961. Retrace your steps and stride on along the shore path to cross the footbridge over the River Ehen. Beyond, turn right and walk on to take the path, on the right, into the car park.

From 1864 Ennerdale's water was used as a water supply for West Cumbria. In 1902 the shallow weir was added to maintain the water level. In 1960, a £700,000 scheme was devised to raise the level by 1.3m to get an extra 6 million gallons of water a day. This would have drowned the Anglers' Inn, which enjoyed a glorious site right on the edge of lake. The inn was owned first by Whitehaven Corporation and then by South Cumberland Water Board. In 1961 they decided the inn should be demolished in order for the scheme to go ahead. The inn was demolished, but the scheme to raise the water level failed. In 1980, North West Water tried again to raise the level by 1.2m for use by BFNL Sellafield and the chemical works at Whitehaven. Michael Heseltine, the minister concerned with the inquiry at the time, refused planning permission. The Anglers' Inn had been demolished to no purpose.

Dr Martin Varley in his book 'Wild Lakeland' describes a remarkable experiment being undertaken in Ennerdale. He says "... the three main landowners, the National Trust, the Forestry Commission and United Utilities have stepped back from managing the valley to let natural processes shape its landscape and wildlife. Wild Ennerdale as the project is known, is a long-term vision for a more wild Lakeland over a whole valley that will conserve it important habitats and inspire those who visit.

7

COGRA MOSS (SHORT WALK)

*As you reach the brow of the track leading to Cogra Moss you have
a delightful view of the reservoir. Once it supplied drinking water for
Alecdon but now it is a fishing lake, very popular with anglers, who
stand in the shallow water casting their lines. The Moss, an attractive
stretch of water, blends so well that it appears completely natural. It
is well sheltered by a horseshoe of fine hills, their lower slopes clad in
conifers, many planted in the 1960s.*

Start/Finish: Car park at Felldyke (GR 088198), which lies nearly
2 miles north of Croasdale, north of Ennerdale Water.
Distance: 4.5km (2¾ miles)
Height gain: Virtually none
Difficulty: Generally flat walking. Small patches of the path or track
can be very muddy, but go where other people have walked.

---

1. Leave the car park by the top right corner and ascend the reinforced
way. At the junction turn left and a very short way along, on the right,
take the signposted small kissing gate beside a large padlocked one,
and continue gently up the fell slope on a wider reinforced track, with
a splendid view of the hills ahead. Go through the next kissing gate,
and carry on the good track, where there has been some clear-felling.
On the now level track you can look down over the ancient wall into
a very deep trough through which flows Rakegill Beck. Very soon you
have a fine view of the reservoir, through some enormous beeches, as
you begin descend.

2. Pass through a large ornate gate on the left, or go over the stile, to
join a path across the overflow from the Moss. Carry on along the dam
to a ladder-stile. Beyond, walk on a narrow path edging the water and

with a fence to your left. Take care on the planks over a wet areas. At a hawthorn tree the fence winds right and the top bar has been removed. Climb over and walk ahead on a fine grassy trod. Half way towards the forest ahead, turn right, following a deer fence on your right. Enjoy the view of the high fells and the reservoir as you go.

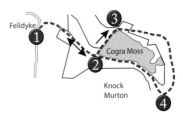

> *The reservoir is not a natural lake. It was formed when the outflow, Rakegill Beck, from Cogra Moss, once a marsh, was dammed. Some of the surrounding conifer forest has been recently clear-felled and, at the time of writing, there has not been enough time for nature to start colonising the slopes. Some of the machinery used for this work has churned up short parts of the tracks, but generally this has been kept to a minimum.*

3. Follow the path over an open area beside deer fencing and then continue along the side of the unfenced conifer forest on your right. Follow the path as it winds steadily right and continues along a wide ride through trees on either side. Ahead stands Lamplugh Fell. Where the path seems to disappear you may have to do a bit of bog hopping until the path quickly reappears. If it soon becomes boggy again, keep to the right side of the path, walking where others have used the rushes to keep dryshod.

4. Go on winding steadily right and aim for an obvious good path that takes you above the head of the reservoir and from where you can see the fishermen – still in the water. Follow the good path as it rises gently. Then join a wider track and follow it right, beside the water. There is more clear-fell here and a bit more mud. Press on through the area, where the fishermen park, and from now on the tracks become easy and quite dry to walk. Very soon you reach the foot of the reservoir and from here retrace your outward route to the parking area.

8

COGRA MOSS SOUTH

This second walk in this pleasing area is longer and ascends part way up the surrounding slopes, with fine views down to the lake.
For much of the way it uses the red coloured forest road, where you might find little lumps of haematite. This is reached by a narrow path that slants up the lower slopes of bulky Knock Murton.

> **Start/Finish:** From Felldyke car park (see walk 7)
> **Distance:** 7.5km (4½ miles)
> **Height gain:** 70m (230ft)
> **Difficulty:** Generally easy walking on paths and tracks.
> The climb up from Cogra Moss ascends steadily –
> take your time and stand still to enjoy the view.

1. Leave the car park by the top right hand corner and go on up the continuing track. Turn left at the junction and, in a few steps, go through the kissing gate, on the right, beside a locked farm gate. Stride up the reinforced track through the meadow and with a splendid view ahead. Go through the next gate, and walk on through clear-fell and under some fine beeches. Descend gently to the reservoir below and pause to enjoy the shimmering lake and perhaps watch the anglers fishing for trout.

2. Stroll on along the right side of the water. Just after the foot of the reservoir, take a narrow but distinct path slanting up the slope. Now that the trees have been felled, heather and bilberry are thriving on what was once the woodland floor. Soon the path comes beside conifer woodland, on the right, before continuing upwards to reach the wide forest road.

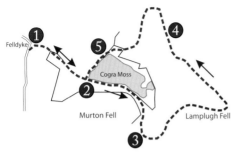

3. Walk left along the pleasingly surfaced way and continue as it traverses Lamplugh Fell, with good views down to the fishing lake. Stroll on where it sometimes passes through dense woodland, or clear-fell, and where it crosses gills, with hurrying becks, racing to reach the reservoir. At the Y-junction of tracks, a mile and a half from where you joined it, keep to the left hand branch and carry on with conifers to the right and an open area to the left, where young larch thrive.

4. Follow the track as it curves round left and then left again to come up against mature larch to the right and the young trees, guarded by a deer fence, to the left. At the end of the woodland, wind right and walk on to reach a fence. Walk left, beside it, and keep on to climb a low section of an ancient iron fence, below a hawthorn tree. Wind right now beside the reservoir and bear left towards the water a short way along. Take care as you cross short planks of wood put down over the muddiest sections. At the right corner of the dam, climb the ladder-stile or squeeze through the gap to its right.

5. Walk on along the dam where you will want to pause to watch the anglers, if present. Cross the bridge over the outflow, the water racing down a concrete chute to hurry on through Rakegill. Go through a large iron gate, turn right and retrace your steps to the car park.

> *Deposits of the rich red haematite iron ore were exploited by the Romans. Knock Murton, the huge bulky fell to your right at the start of the walk, was studded with mines. These were large producers of the ore and, between 1869 and 1913, over 1.25 million tons were raised and transported away from the mine by a railway line.*

9

SMITHY BECK FOREST TRAIL

The Trail combines a pleasing walk beside Ennerdale Water with a waymarked route continuing through the forest. Clearings, carpeted with heather thriving between outcrops of rock, reveal wonderful views of the surrounding fells. The walk takes you along narrow up-and-down paths, comes near to a 'secret' clearing – once the site of a medieval settlement – and visits two magnificent viewpoints overlooking the lake. The trail divides into two parts. The shorter takes about an hour at a steady pace and the full trail, twice as long, explores higher parts.

Start/Finish: Bowness Knott car park (NY109154).
This lies on the north side of Ennerdale Water at the end of
the road; vehicles are not allowed beyond the car park.
To access this from the village of Ennerdale Bridge take the narrow
road leading towards the lake. Where the road divides take
the left fork and continue on the winding way to Croasdale,
where you turn right. The parking area lies
6km (3¾ miles) from the village.
Distance: Shorter walk 3.4km (2 miles);
Longer walk 5.8km (3½ miles)
Height gain: 160m (525ft)
Difficulty: Moderate climbs on paths that can be muddy after rain.

Holly, juniper oak, rowan, birch and hawthorn grow between the taller trees. On the floor of the forest look for lichens, liverworts and mosses. The trees form a blanket over them, trapping warmth, raising the moisture in the air and protecting them from the wind.

1. Leave the car park and walk on along the wide track towards the

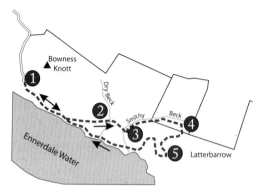

head of the lake. At the first small picnic site, take the signposted trail, climbing left through trees. Turn right along a wide forest ride bordered with larch on the right and Scots pine growing on the steeper slopes to your left. Follow the gently climbing ride to come to the side of Dry Beck. It is given this name because what water it does have percolates through the boulders of the bed and is lost to sight. Where the water empties into the lake you can hear it hurrying below the rocks, but again there is generally nothing to be seen.

2. Cross the footbridge and stride on, still ascending. Look out for where the trail leaves the forest road, makes a sharp right turn and descends to the side of Smithy Beck. The trail divides here and if you wish to return at this point, ignore the footbridge over the beck and descend to the lakeside, where you turn right to return to the car park.

3. To continue on the longer walk, cross the footbridge and pause to enjoy the splendid waterfall to your left. Then climb the opposite bank of Smithy Beck to turn left along a track to the forest road, where you turn left again. Then you come to an area of peat moorland and where the forest road divides and turns left or right, look for a narrow path, with a notice board, continuing ahead into a clearing to see the remains of the medieval settlement.

> *The medieval settlement was occupied by farmers who also mined for iron ore. The original forest of oak,*

alder, birch and hazel was felled by them to produce the charcoal they needed to smelt the ores. They produced the charcoal by slow 'burning' in pitsteads scattered through the forest. The charcoal was then carried by ponies to the mouth of Smithy Beck, where the iron was smelted in a bloomery.

4. Go on almost to the end of the clearing and then turn right to climb a wide grassy ride through a plantation, originally of lodgepole pine. During a storm in 1984 gale force winds blew many down. The area has been re-planted with larch and deciduous trees. As you climb notice the tiny feathery plants growing on the larch. These are lichens and they thrive in the pure, damp air. The lovely way continues to a splendid viewpoint where a notice board tells you the 'Ennerdale Story'. If the sun is shining this is the place for a picnic.

5. Descend the well graded path, over the shoulder of Latterbarrow, towards the lake. Pause to enjoy the spectacular views. Cross a forest road and then follow a path to join the main track beside the lake. Turn right to return to the car park. As you go look for pieces of slag on the shore at the mouth of Smithy Beck, all that remains of the bloomery and listen for the hidden water of Dry Beck.

Almost at the start of the second part of the walk, you have climbed steadily until you are now above the 183m contour line, where in the north and west of the British Isles high rainfall is expected and not much sunshine to dry it up. The rain takes the goodness out of the soil and carries both down the steep slopes, causing erosion and leaving the soil acid. This is poor soil for farming but it can grow some very good trees if it is ploughed and given back some nutrients.

31

10

LIZA BECK

The Liza Beck rises on the slopes of Great Gable and hurries all the way, over fell and then through forest, to Ennerdale Water. This walk crosses the Liza at Gillerthwaite footbridge, and goes on over pastureland. It then follows a waymarked trail, which has been constructed beside the river on its southern side. It continues through the forest to cross the river again by a concrete bridge, and then returns along the forest road on the northern side of the river.

Start/Finish: Bowness Knott car park (NY109154)
Distance: 11.4km (7 miles)
Height gain: 150m (495ft)
Difficulty: Easy walking on wide tracks and footpaths

---

1. Leave the car park and continue along the forest road, with the lake to your right, for just over 2.5km (1½ miles) to pass, on your right, the concrete bridge spanning Char Dub – which you ignore. Carry on to descend a slope, right, to cross Gillerthwaite footbridge over the River Liza. Turn left, go over a stile and, keeping a wall to your right, go on to climb another stile. Continue on to cross the Little Irish Bridge and walk on for a few steps along the forest track, now on the southern side of the river. Here go through a hand gate to the left of the gate across the track to walk a glorious path that goes off left and leads you on between the river and the forest track.

> *Tree planting in Ennerdale started in 1926 to help create a reserve of timber and to provide work for the unemployed miners of Cleator Moor. Today, as areas are cleared of conifers, Forest Enterprise hopes to plant a much greater variety of trees and to leave far more open spaces.*

As you walk through the forest you might see roe deer. These small mammals browse the tops of pine shoots, leaving frayed edges. They also graze yew and gorse. Their droppings, black to dark brown and deposited in heaps, are easily confused with those of sheep.

2. Look out for Moss Dub, a tarn on your right, edged with birch and rhododendrons. Towards the end of the pretty sheet of water, descend steps on your left. Stride on to the side of Low Beck and walk right. Do not be confused by the small footbridge ahead, which is on the opposite bank of the river and cannot be reached. At the forest track, bear left, cross a bridge and turn immediately left to walk the opposite bank of Low Beck then cross the footbridge seen earlier.

3. Stroll on, with a dramatic view of Pillar mountain ahead, to reach the side of High Beck. As with Low Beck, walk right, beside the stream, before crossing a footbridge. Beyond bear left and press on beside the Liza with its many rocky pools and small waterfalls. Eventually you join the forest track, where you wind left to cross a concrete bridge to the northern side of the Liza.

4. Turn left and begin your return along the wide forest road, enjoying the magnificent views as you go. Continue past the Char Dubb Bridge to pick up the

Gillerthwaite

Moss Dub

Lingmell Plantations

River Liza

Bowness Knott

Ennerdale Water

footpath, on the left of the road until it returns you to the road again. Carry on beside the lake. As you near the car park, the road climbs away, right, from the lake.

Golden Rules for Safe Walking, even on Easy Rambles, and the Countryside Code

Wear suitable clothes and take adequate waterproofs.

In summer wear a hat and take sufficient drinking water

Walk in strong footwear; walking boots or shoes are advisable.

Carry the relevant map and a compass and know how to use them.

Carry a torch in the winter months

Carry a whistle; remember six long blasts repeated at one minute intervals is the distress signal.

Do not walk alone, and if you do, tell someone where you are going.

If mist descends, return.

Be safe and plan ahead.

Leave gates and property as you find them.

Protect plants and animals and take your litter home.

Keep dogs under close control.

Consider other people.

Keep all dogs under strict control. Observe all 'No Dogs' notices – they are there for good reason.

Other titles by
QUESTA PUBLISHING LIMITED

LAKE DISTRICT
WALKS WITH CHILDREN
Buttermere and the Vale of Lorton
Around Coniston
Keswick and the Newlands Valley
Ambleside
Grasmere
Ullswater
Around Kendal
Around Windermere
South Lakeland

EASY RAMBLES
Around Keswick and Borrowdale
Around Ambleside and Grasmere
Around Eskdale
Around Wasdale
Around Dunnerdale
Around Coniston and Hawkshead
Around Patterdale and Ullswater
Around Langdale

YORKSHIRE DALES
WALKS WITH CHILDREN
Wharfedale
Swaledale
Wensleydale
Malham and Airedale
Ribblesdale

PEAK DISTRICT
WALKS WITH CHILDREN
Dark Peak

PENNINES
SHORT WALKS
Eden Valley and North Pennines

All QUESTA titles are available from
27 Camwood, BAMBER BRIDGE, Lancashire PR5 8LA
or by FAX to
0705 349 1743

www.questapublishing.co.uk